PREP LEVEL Supplemental
ANSWER BOOK

By Glory St. Germain ARCT RMT MYCC UMTC &
Shelagh McKibbon-U'Ren RMT UMTC

The PREP LEVEL Supplemental Workbook is designed to be completed with the Prep 1 Rudiments Workbook.

GSG MUSIC
Enriching Lives Through Music Education

ISBN: 978-1-927641-51-4

# The Ultimate Music Theory™ Program

The Ultimate Music Theory™ Program lays the foundation of music theory education.

The focus of the Ultimate Music Theory Program is to simplify complex concepts and show the relativity of these concepts with practical application. This program is designed to help teachers and students discover the excitement and benefits of a sound music theory education.

The Ultimate Music Theory Program is based on a proven approach to the study of music theory that follows the *"must have"* Learning Principles to develop effective learning for all learning styles.

The Ultimate Music Theory™ Program and Supplemental Workbooks help students prepare for nationally recognized theory examinations including the Royal Conservatory of Music.

Respect Copyright - Copyright 2017 Gloryland Publishing
All rights reserved. No part of this publication may be reproduced or transmitted in any form or by any means, electronic or mechanical, including photocopying, recording, or any information storage and retrieval system, without permission in writing from the author/publisher.

* Resources - An annotated list is available at UltimateMusicTheory.com under Free Resources.

Library and Archives Canada Cataloguing in Publication
UMT Supplemental Series / Glory St. Germain and Shelagh McKibbon-U'Ren

Gloryland Publishing - UMT Supplemental Series Answer Books:

GP-SPLA	ISBN: 978-1-927641-51-4	UMT Supplemental Prep Level Answer Book
GP-SL1A	ISBN: 978-1-927641-52-1	UMT Supplemental Level 1 Answer Book
GP-SL2A	ISBN: 978-1-927641-53-8	UMT Supplemental Level 2 Answer Book
GP-SL3A	ISBN: 978-1-927641-54-5	UMT Supplemental Level 3 Answer Book
GP-SL4A	ISBN: 978-1-927641-55-2	UMT Supplemental Level 4 Answer Book
GP-SL5A	ISBN: 978-1-927641-56-9	UMT Supplemental Level 5 Answer Book
GP-SL6A	ISBN: 978-1-927641-57-6	UMT Supplemental Level 6 Answer Book
GP-SL7A	ISBN: 978-1-927641-58-3	UMT Supplemental Level 7 Answer Book
GP-SL8A	ISBN: 978-1-927641-59-0	UMT Supplemental Level 8 Answer Book
GP-SCLA	ISBN: 978-1-927641-60-6	UMT Supplemental Complete Level Answer Book

Ultimate Music Theory
PREP LEVEL Supplemental

Table of Contents

Ultimate Music Theory	The Story of UMT… Meet So-La & Ti-Do	4
Comparison Chart	Preparatory Level	6
Ledger Lines	Treble Staff and Bass Staff	8
Pitch and Steps	Treble Staff and Bass Staff	10
Ledger Lines	Grand Staff	12
Middle C and Skips	Grand Staff	13
Pitch and Direction	Same, Different, Direction Arrows	14
C Major Scale	Ascend & Descend, Degrees and Tonic	18
A Minor Scale	Natural form and Tonic	20
Musical Terms & Signs	Dynamics, Articulation and Game	22
Melody Writing	Motive, Repetition and Composition (ICE)	24
Analysis	Sight Reading - Popcorn Dance	27
Music History	Time Periods and Instruments	28
Theory Exam	Preparatory Level	30
Certificate	Completion of Preparatory Level	40

Score: 60 - 69 Pass;   70 - 79 Honors;   80 - 89 First Class Honors;   90 - 100 First Class Honors with Distinction

Ultimate Music Theory: *The Way to Score Success!*

Workbooks, Exams, Answers, Online Courses, App & More!

A Proven Step-by-Step System to Learn Theory Faster - from Beginner to Advanced.

Innovative techniques designed to develop a complete understanding of music theory, to enhance sight reading, ear training, creativity, composition and musical expression.

All UMT Series have matching Answer Books!

The UMT Rudiments Series - Beginner A, Beginner B, Beginner C, Prep 1, Prep 2, Basic, Intermediate, Advanced & Complete (All-In-One)

- ♪ 12 Lessons, Review Tests, and a Final Exam to develop confidence
- ♪ Music Theory Guide & Chart for fast and easy reference of theory concepts
- ♪ 80 Flashcards for fun drills to dramatically increase retention & comprehension

Rudiments Exam Series - Preparatory, Basic, Intermediate & Advanced

- ♪ 8 Exams plus UMT Tips on How to Score 100% on Theory Exams

Each Rudiments Workbook correlates to a Supplemental Workbook.

The UMT Supplemental Series - Prep Level, Level 1, Level 2, Level 3, Level 4, Level 5, Level 6, Level 7, Level 8 & Complete (All-In-One) Level

- ♪ Form & Analysis and Music History - Composers, Eras & Musical Styles
- ♪ Melody Writing using ICE - Imagine, Compose & Explore
- ♪ 12 Lessons, Review Tests, Final Exam and 80 Flashcards for quick study

Supplemental Exam Series - Level 5, Level 6, Level 7 & Level 8

- ♪ 8 Exams to successfully prepare for nationally recognized Theory Exams

UMT Online Courses, Music Theory App & More

- ♪ UMT Certification Course, Teachers Membership & Elite Educator Program
- ♪ Ultimate Music Theory App correlates to the Rudiments Workbooks
- ♪ Free Resources - Teachers Guide, Music Theory Blogs, videos & downloads

Go To: **UltimateMusicTheory.com**

At Ultimate Music Theory we are passionate about helping teachers and students experience the joy of teaching and learning music by creating the most effective music theory materials on the planet!

Introducing the Ultimate Music Theory Family!

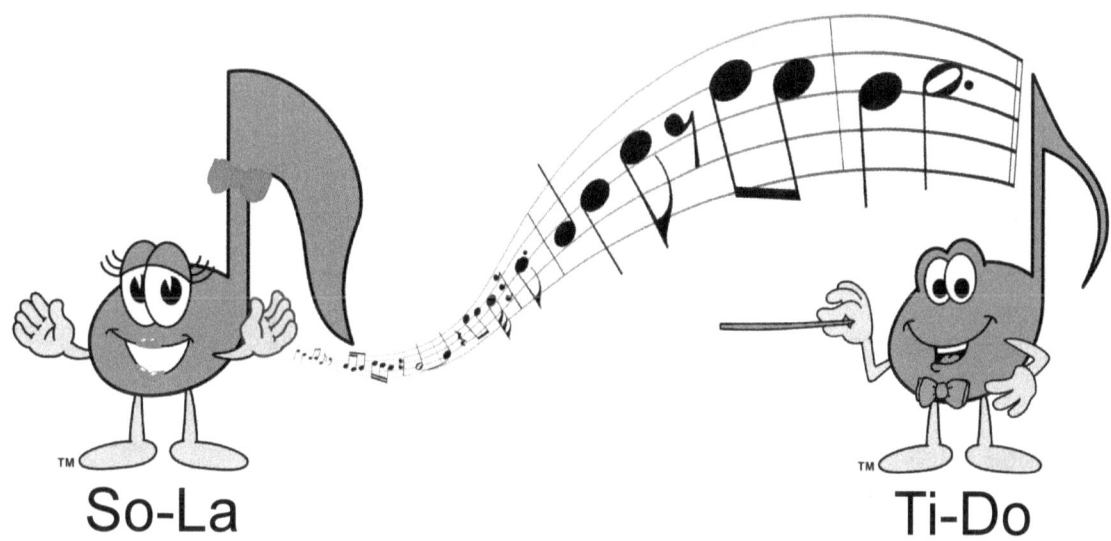

So-La

Meet So-La! So-La loves to sing and dance.

She is expressive, creative and loves to tell stories through music!

So-La feels music in her heart. She loves to teach, compose and perform.

Ti-Do

Meet Ti-Do! Ti-Do loves to count and march.

He is rhythmic, consistent and loves the rules of music theory!

Ti-Do feels music in his hands and feet. He loves to analyze, share tips and conduct.

So-La & Ti-Do will guide you through Mastering Music Theory!

Enriching Lives Through Music Education

The Ultimate Music Theory™ Comparison Chart to the 2016 Royal Conservatory of Music Theory Syllabus.
Preparatory Level

The Ultimate Music Theory™ Rudiments Workbooks, Supplemental Workbooks and Exams prepare students for successful completion of the Royal Conservatory of Music Theory Levels.

UMT Prep 1 Rudiments Workbook plus the PREP LEVEL Supplemental = RCM Preparatory Level.
♪ Note: Additional completion of the LEVEL 1 Supplemental Workbook = RCM Theory Level 1.

RCM Preparatory Theory Concept

Required Keys
- C Major and a minor

Pitch and Notation
- Staff: Treble Clef, Bass Clef & Grand Staff

- Bar Lines and Measures
- Notes up to and including one ledger line above and below the Treble & Bass Staff
- Notes adjacent to Middle C on the Treble & Bass Staff
- Location of notes on a keyboard diagram
(No Accidentals)

Rhythm and Meter
- Notes: whole, half, quarter and eighth
- Rests: whole, half, quarter and eighth
- Time Signatures: 2/4 and 4/4

Intervals
- Notes moving by step, by skip or that repeat

Scales and Scale Degree Names
(No Pentascales)

- C Major Scale and a minor natural scale

- Scale Degree Names: Tonic

Ultimate Music Theory Prep 1 Workbook

Keys Covered
- C Major and a minor; F Major and d minor; G Major and e minor

Pitch and Notation Covered
- Staff: Treble Clef, Bass Clef & Grand Staff
* Workbook page - Middle C and Skips - Grand Staff
* Workbook page - Same Pitch, Different Staff
* Workbook page - Same Letter Names - Different Pitches
- Bar Lines (Single & Double) and Measures
- Notes on the Treble & Bass Staff
* Workbook page - Ledger Lines - Grand Staff
* Workbook page - Ledger Lines - Treble Staff
* Workbook page - Ledger Lines - Bass Staff
- Location of notes on a keyboard diagram
- Accidentals: Sharp, Flat and Natural

Rhythm and Meter Covered
- Notes: whole, dotted half, half, quarter and eighth
- Rests: whole, half, quarter and eighth
- Time Signatures: 2/4, 3/4 and 4/4

Intervals Covered
- Notes moving by step, by skip or that repeat
* Workbook page - Pitch and Steps - Treble Staff
* Workbook page - Pitch and Steps - Bass Staff
* Workbook page - Direction Arrows, Same and Steps
* Workbook page - Direction Arrows and Skips

Scales and Scale Degree Names Covered
- Pentascales: C Major and a minor, F Major and d minor, G Major and e minor
* Workbook page - C Major Scale
* Workbook page - a minor Scale, Natural Form
- Scale Degree Names: Tonic, Mediant and Dominant
* Workbook page - C Major Scale and the Tonic
* Workbook page - a minor Scale, Natural Form, and the Tonic

* Supplemental Workbook Pages - New concepts introduced in the 2016 RCM Syllabus.

UltimateMusicTheory.com © Copyright 2017 Gloryland Publishing. All Rights Reserved.

RCM Preparatory Theory Concept (Continued)

Chords
- Tonic Triad of C Major and of a minor (Root Position, solid/blocked and broken)

Music Terms and Signs
- Dynamics and Articulation Terms/Signs

Analysis
(No Analysis Questions)

Melody Writing and Composition
(No Melody Writing Questions)
(No Composition Questions)

Music History
(No Music History Questions)

Examination
(No Preparatory Level Theory Exam)

Ultimate Music Theory Prep 1 Workbook (Continued)

Chords Covered
- Tonic Triad of C Major, a minor, F Major, d minor, G Major and e minor (Root Position, solid/blocked and broken)

Music Terms and Signs Covered
- Dynamics, Articulation and Tempo Terms/Signs
* Workbook page - Musical Terms and Signs
* Game - Climb the Beanstock

Analysis
- Analysis Questions in each Review Test
* Workbook page - Analysis and Sight Reading

Melody Writing and Composition
* Workbook page - Melody Writing
* Workbook page - Motive - A Musical Idea
* Workbook page - Imagine, Compose, Explore

Music History
* Workbook page - Music History - Time Periods and Instruments

Review Tests & Final Exam
- 12 Accumulative Review Tests (1 with each of the 12 Lessons)
* UMT PREPARATORY LEVEL THEORY EXAM

UltimateMusicTheoryApp.com - 6 Subjects: Beginner - Prep, Basic, Intermediate, Advanced, Ear Training & Music Trivia (including History).

The Ultimate Music Theory Flashcards App (Powered by Brainscape) is a fun and amazing learning tool! With Over 7000 Flashcards in the UMT App - and the ONLY App with matching workbooks - it's easy to see, hear and learn faster!

Beginner Music Theory App Subject - Use with the Prep 1 and Prep 2 Workbooks

12 Decks - 1,325 Cards - See, hear and identify notes on the staff, scales, triads and musical terms. Learn notation including note and rest values, Key Signatures, 4/4 Simple Time & more!

1 - Notation, Landmarks and Ledger Lines
2 - Note & Rest Values and Intervals
3 - Simple Time Signatures
4 - Semitones, Whole tones & Accidentals
5 - Major scales - 2 sharps & 2 flats
6 - Natural minor scales - 2 sharps & 2 flats
7 - Key Signatures - 2 sharps & 2 flats
8 - Key Signatures on the Grand Staff
9 - Major Triads - solid and broken
10 - Harmonic minor scales
11 - Melodic minor scales
12 - Analysis and Musical Terms

LEDGER LINES - TREBLE STAFF (Use after Prep 1 Workbook Page 19)

Ledger lines are short lines used to extend the staff as needed for notes written above or below the Treble Clef. Ledger lines must be equal distance from the staff.

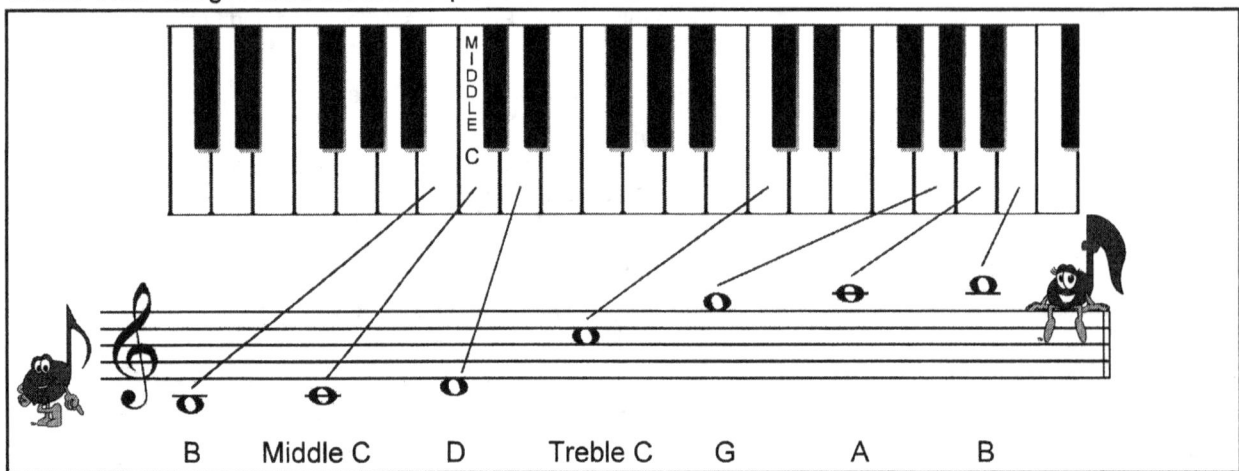

1. a) Copy the following notes below and above the Treble Clef.
   b) Name the notes.

B   C   D   B   C   D   G   A   B   G   A   B

2. Write the following notes. Use ledger lines when needed. Use whole notes.

   a) ABOVE the Treble Clef.

   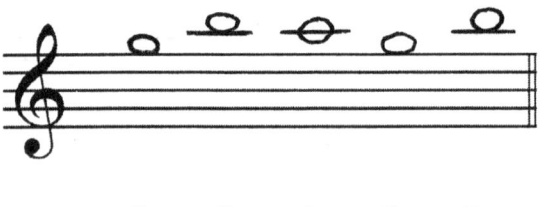

   G   B   A   G   B

   b) BELOW the Treble Clef.

   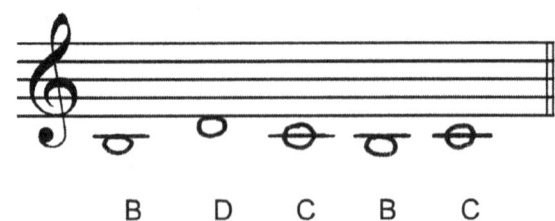

   B   D   C   B   C

3. Name the following notes in the Treble Clef.

C   A   G   B   B   D   G   C   C

LEDGER LINES - BASS STAFF (Use after Prep 1 Workbook Page 25)

Ledger lines are short lines used to extend the staff as needed for notes written above or below the Bass Clef. Always use your UMT Ruler to draw straight ledger lines.

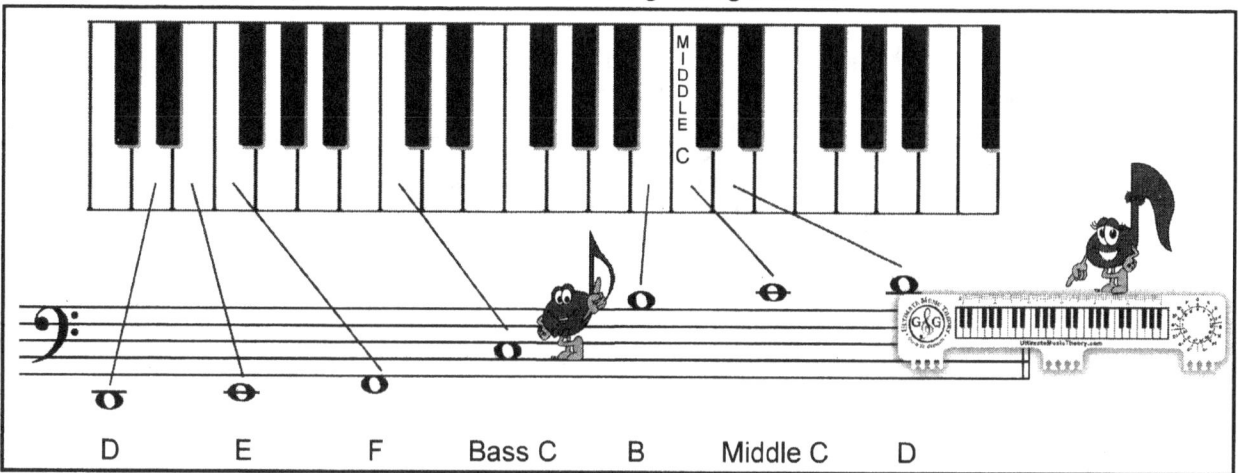

1. a) Copy the following notes below and above the Bass Clef.
   b) Name the notes.

D E F   D E F   B C D   B C D

2. Write the following notes. Use ledger lines when needed. Use whole notes.

   a) ABOVE the Bass Clef.   b) BELOW the Bass Clef.

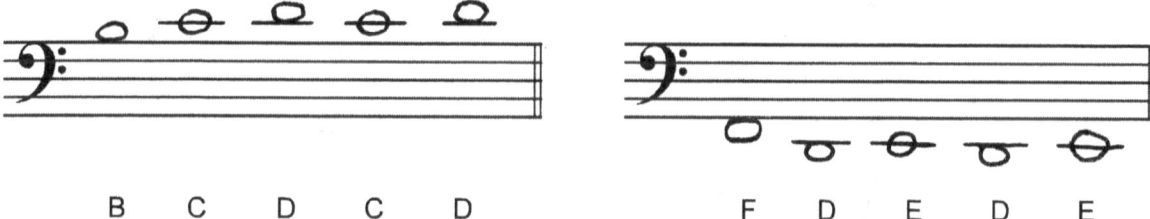

B C D C D   F D E D E

3. Name the following notes in the Bass Clef.

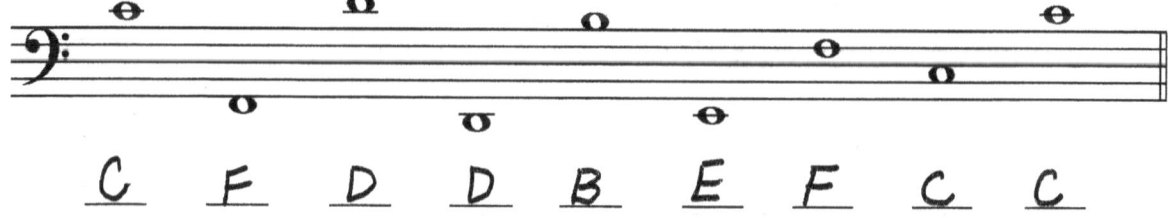

C F D D B E F C C

PITCH and STEPS - TREBLE STAFF (Use after Prep 1 Workbook Page 30)

Notes on the Treble Staff correspond to specific **pitches** on the keyboard. Pitch has direction. As the notes move up the Treble Staff (to the right on the keyboard), the sound gets **higher** in pitch.

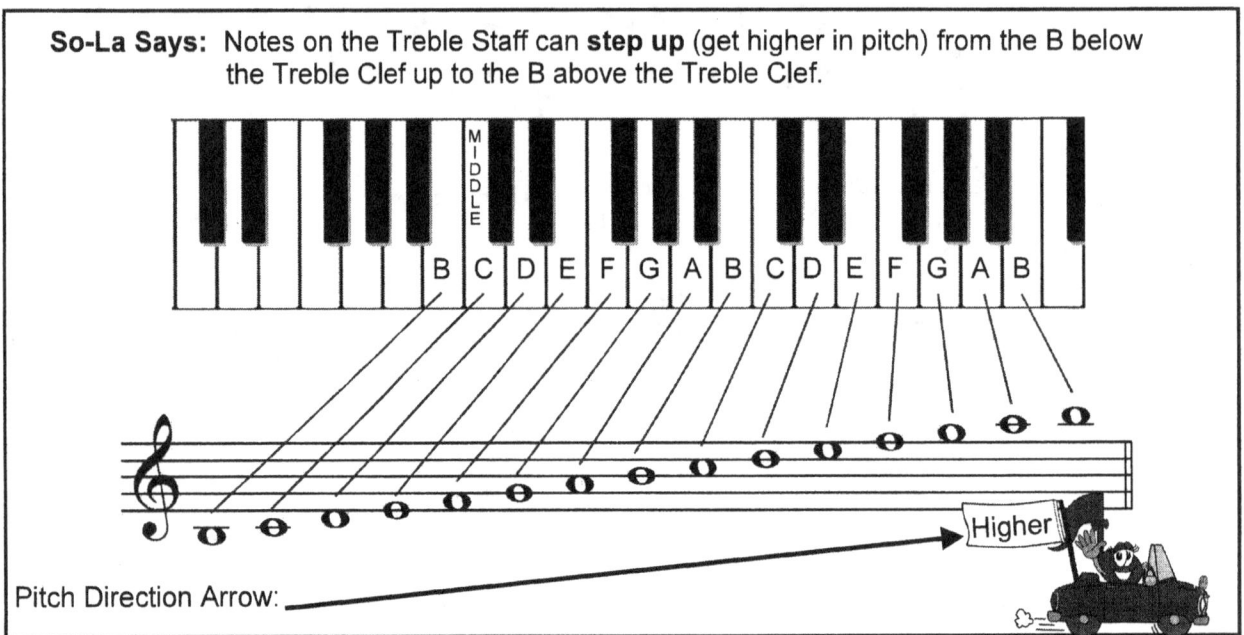

♪ **Ti-Do Tip:** When stepping from one line note to the next space note, or from one space note to the next line note, the pattern is called a step. Notes that step up go higher in pitch. Notes that step down go lower in pitch.

1. a) Name the following notes.
   b) Circle the correct pattern below.

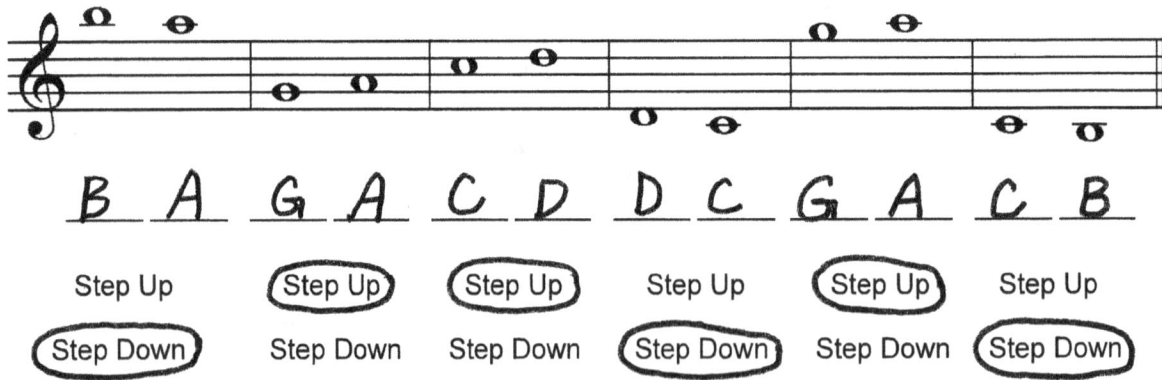

♪ **Ti-Do Time:** PLAY the Treble Clef notes in the Example Box on your instrument. Listen as the pitch gets higher in sound. Play them again; start at the top and go down. Listen as the pitch gets lower in sound.

LISTEN as your Teacher plays the notes in Exercise #1. Without looking at the music, identify if the pitch (sound) is a Step Up or a Step Down.

PITCH and STEPS - BASS STAFF (Use after Prep 1 Workbook Page 30)

Notes on the Bass Staff correspond to specific **pitches** on the keyboard. Pitch has direction. As the notes move up the Bass Staff (to the right on the keyboard), the sound gets **higher** in pitch.

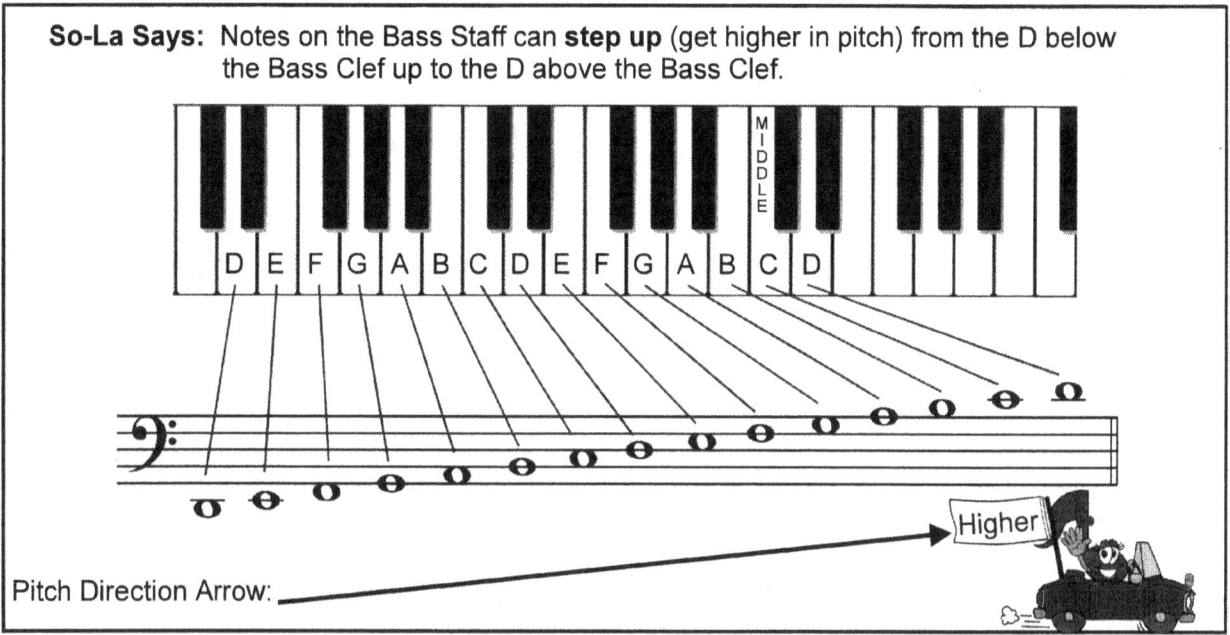

So-La Says: Notes on the Bass Staff can **step up** (get higher in pitch) from the D below the Bass Clef up to the D above the Bass Clef.

Pitch Direction Arrow:

♫ **Ti-Do Tip:** When stepping from one line note to the next space note, or from one space note to the next line note, the pattern is called a step. Notes that step up go higher in pitch. Notes that step down go lower in pitch.

1. a) Name the following notes.
   b) Circle the correct pattern below.

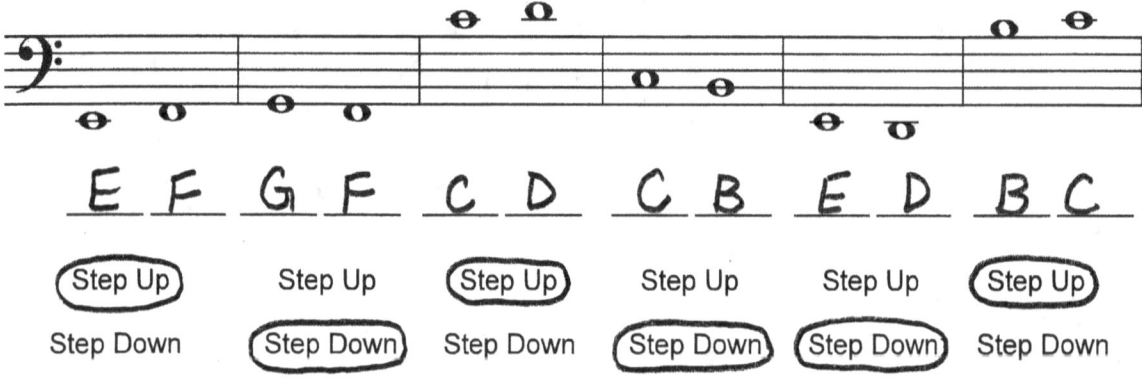

E F   G F   C D   C B   E D   B C

(Step Up)   Step Up   (Step Up)   Step Up   Step Up   (Step Up)

Step Down   (Step Down)   Step Down   (Step Down)   (Step Down)   Step Down

♫ **Ti-Do Time:** PLAY the Bass Clef notes in the Example Box on your instrument. Listen as the pitch gets higher in sound. Play them again; start at the top and go down. Listen as the pitch gets lower in sound.

LISTEN as your Teacher plays the notes in Exercise #1. Without looking at the music, identify if the pitch (sound) is a Step Up or a Step Down.

LEDGER LINES - GRAND STAFF (Use after Prep 1 Rudiments Page 35)

Ledger Lines are used to extend the **Grand Staff**.

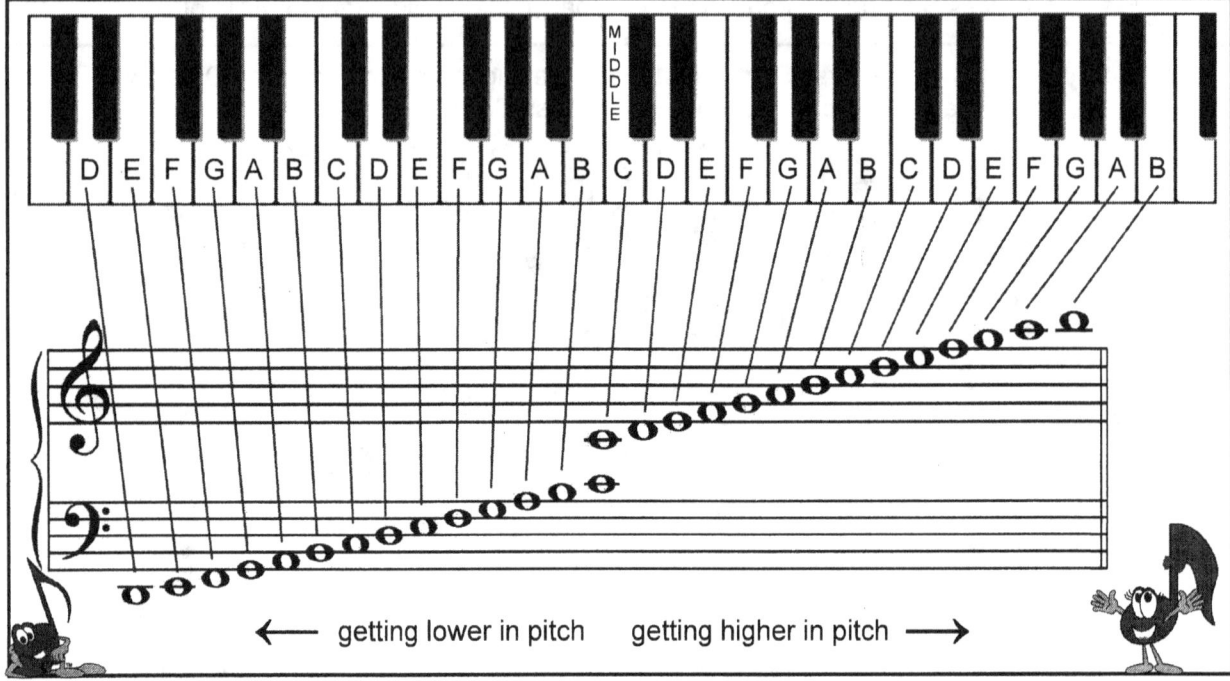

1. a) Write the following notes indicated on the keyboard with a ☺ directly on the Grand Staff below. Use whole notes.
   b) Name the notes.
   c) Draw a line from each note to the corresponding key on the keyboard (at the correct pitch).

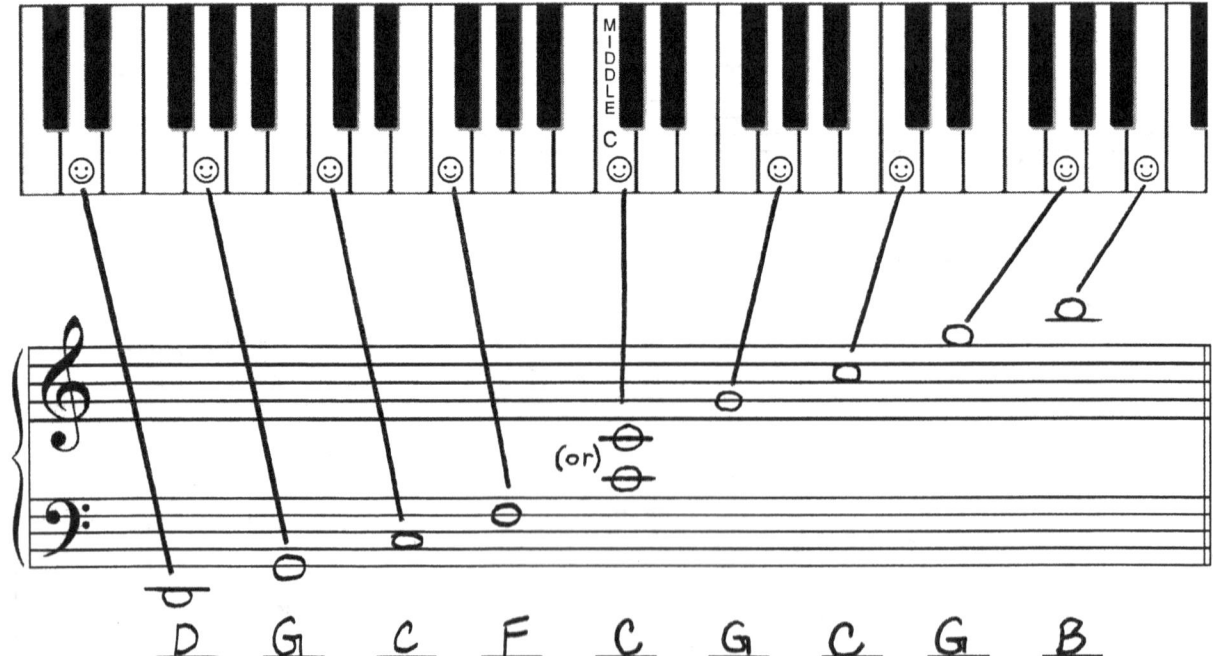

D G C F C G C G B

MIDDLE C and SKIPS - GRAND STAFF (Use after Prep 1 Rudiments Page 35)

On the Grand Staff, **Middle C** is written on a Ledger Line between the Treble Clef and the Bass Clef.

So-La Says: When Middle C is written on the Ledger Line below line 1 of the Treble Clef, it is part of the Treble Staff.

When Middle C is written on the Ledger Line above line 5 of the Bass Clef, it is part of the Bass Staff.

♪ **Ti-Do Tip:** When skipping from one line note to the next line note, or from one space note to the next space note, the pattern is called a skip. Notes that skip up go higher in pitch. Notes that skip down go lower in pitch.

1. a) Name the following notes.
   b) Draw a line from each note to the corresponding key on the keyboard (at the correct pitch).
   c) Name the key directly on the keyboard.

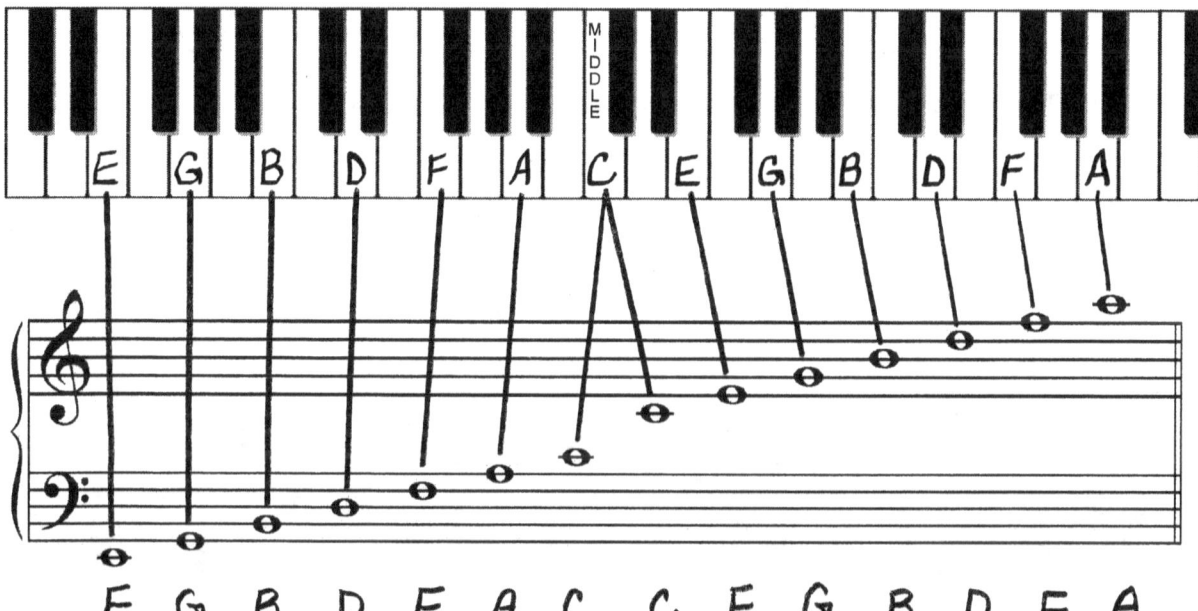

E G B D F A C C E G B D F A

♪ **Ti-Do Time:** PLAY the notes from Exercise #1 on your instrument. Listen as the pitch skips higher in sound. Play them again; start at the top and go down. Listen as the pitch skips lower in sound.

LISTEN as your Teacher plays the notes in Exercise #1. Without looking at the music, identify if the pitch (sound) is a Skip Up or a Skip Down.

UltimateMusicTheory.com © Copyright 2017 Gloryland Publishing. All Rights Reserved.

SAME PITCH, DIFFERENT STAFF (Use after Prep 1 Rudiments Page 35)

Using Ledger Lines, notes can be written at the **same pitch** in the Treble Staff and in the Bass Staff.

♪ **Ti-Do Tip:** The B closest to Middle C can be written in the Bass Staff and in the Treble Staff.
Middle C can be written in the Bass Staff and in the Treble Staff.
The D closest to Middle C can be written in the Bass Staff and in the Treble Staff.

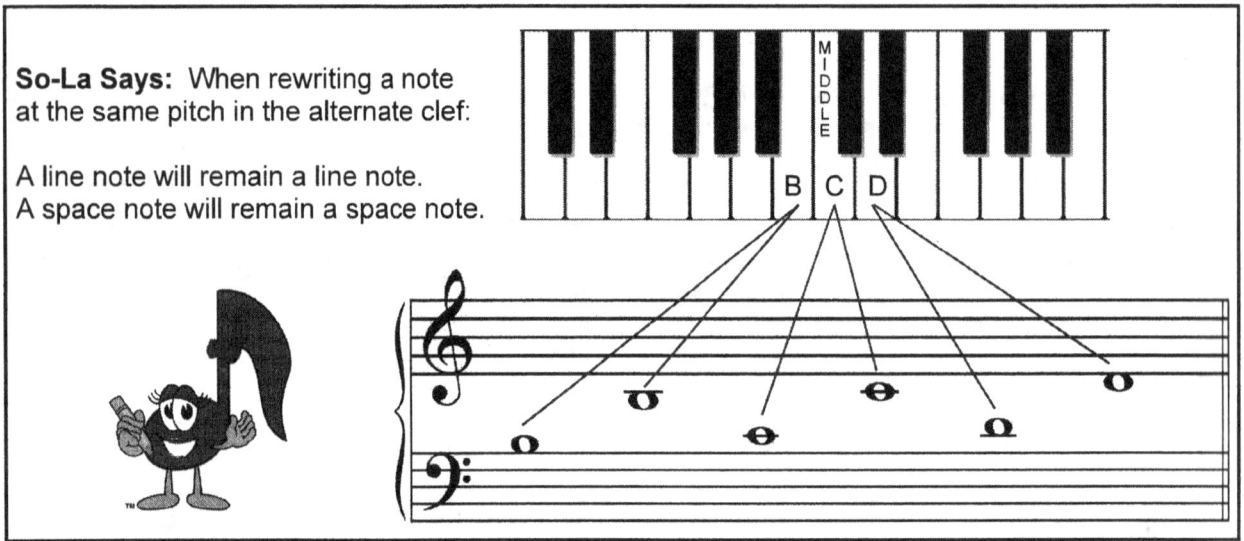

♪ **Ti-Do Tip:** Two notes written at the same pitch but in alternate clefs will sound the same.

1. a) Name the following notes.
   b) Circle the correct pitch pattern below.

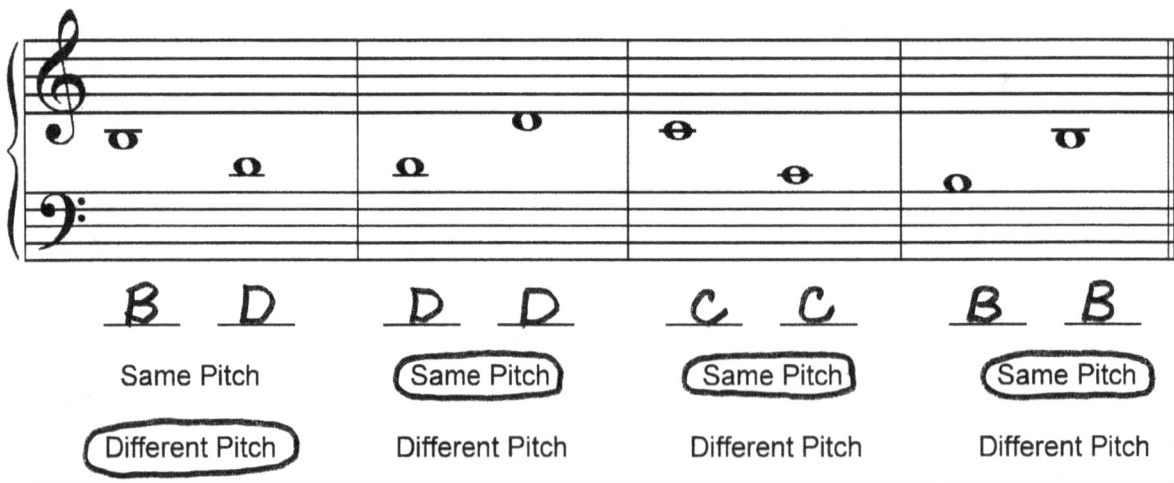

♪ **Ti-Do Time:**

LISTEN as your Teacher plays the 2 note pattern in Exercise #1. Without looking at the music, identify if the pitch (sound) is at the Same Pitch or at a Different Pitch.

DIRECTION ARROWS, SAME and STEPS (Use after Prep 1 Rudiments Page 35)

Direction Arrows identify the pitch - **Same** (repeat), **Up** (getting higher) or **Down** (getting lower).

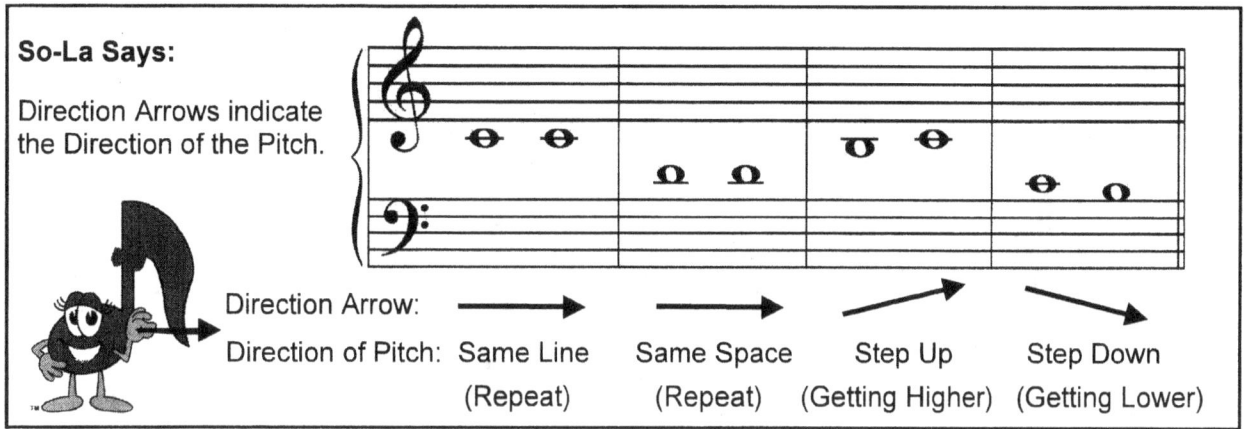

So-La Says:

Direction Arrows indicate the Direction of the Pitch.

♫ **Ti-Do Tip:** When a note is repeated at the same pitch, a line note will go to a note on the same line, and a space note will go to a note in the same space.

1. Following the Direction Arrow, draw a whole note at the same pitch (repeat) as the given note.

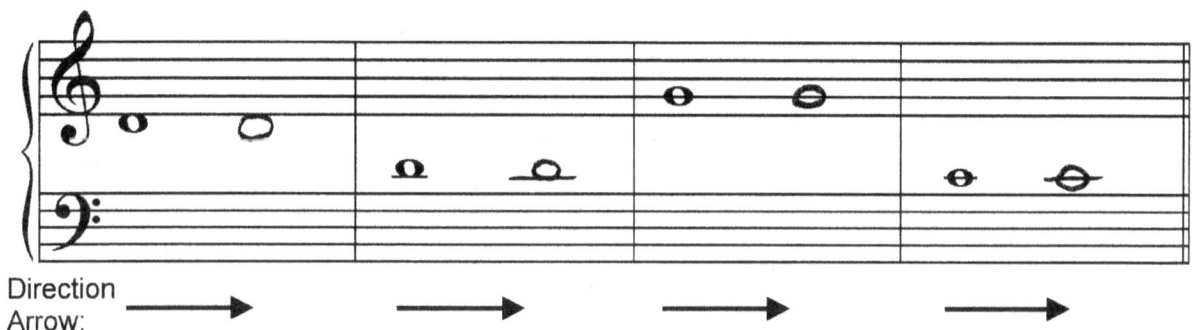

♫ **Ti-Do Tip:** A step is written from a line note to the next space note, or from a space note to the next line note.

2. a) Following the Direction Arrow, draw a whole note a step up or a step down from each note.
   b) Name the notes.

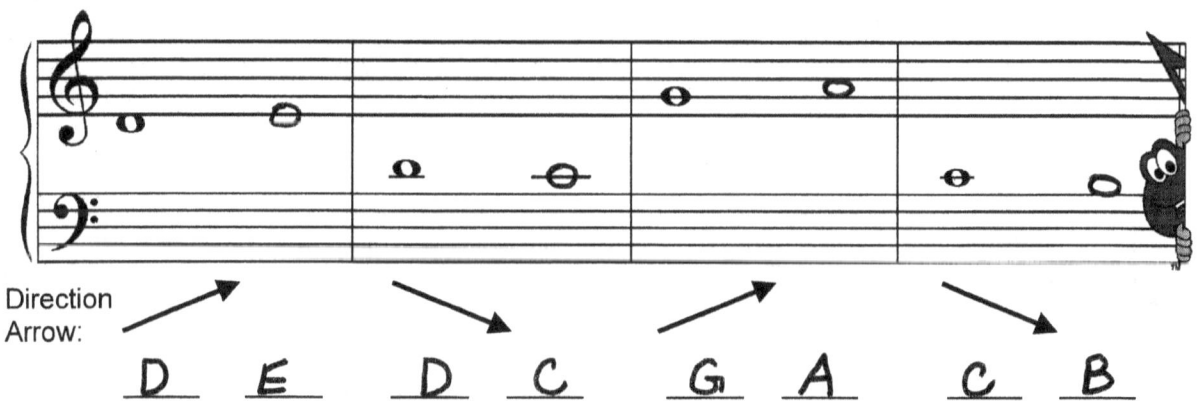

D E   D C   G A   C B

DIRECTION ARROWS and SKIPS (Use after Prep 1 Rudiments Page 35)

Direction Arrows identify the pitch: Same (repeat), Up (getting higher) or Down (getting lower).

The Direction of Pitch can be: Same Line, Same Space, Step Up, Step Down, Skip Up or Skip Down.

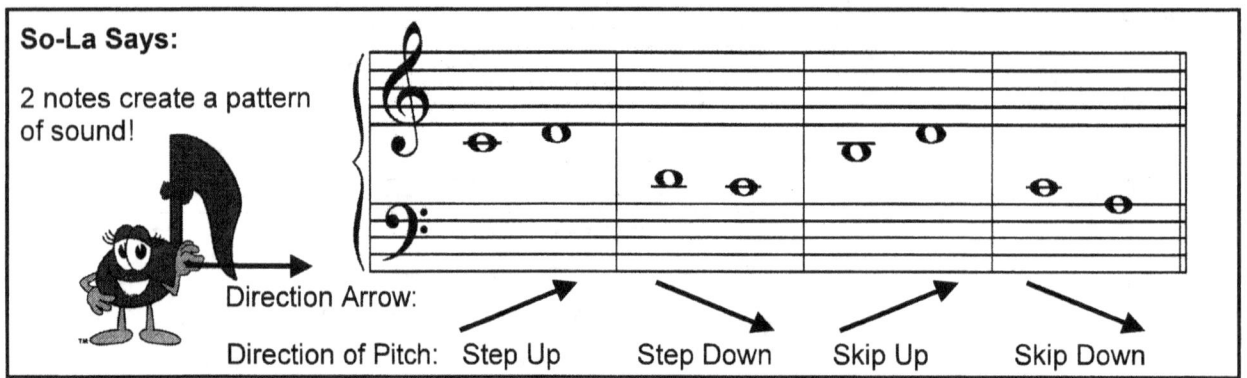

♪ **Ti-Do Tip:** A skip is a line note to the next line note (skipping a space), or a space note to the next space note (skipping a line).

1. a) Following the Direction Arrow, draw a whole note a skip up or a skip down from each note.
   b) Name the notes.

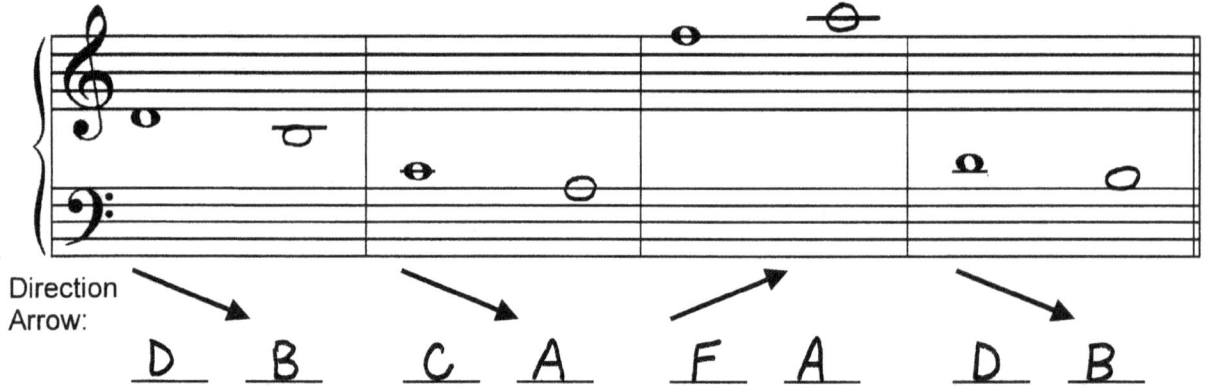

2. a) Name the following notes.
   b) Circle the correct pattern (pitch direction) below each measure.

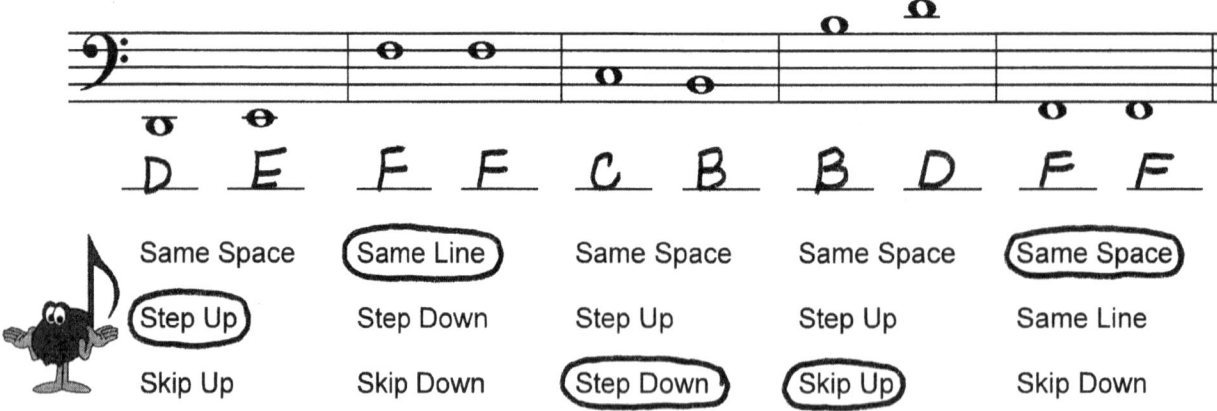

SAME LETTER NAMES - DIFFERENT PITCHES (Use after Prep 1 Rudiments Page 35)

Each letter name of the Musical Alphabet can be written at **different pitches** on the Grand Staff.

The letter names B, C and D can be written at the same pitch but in the alternate (other) clef.

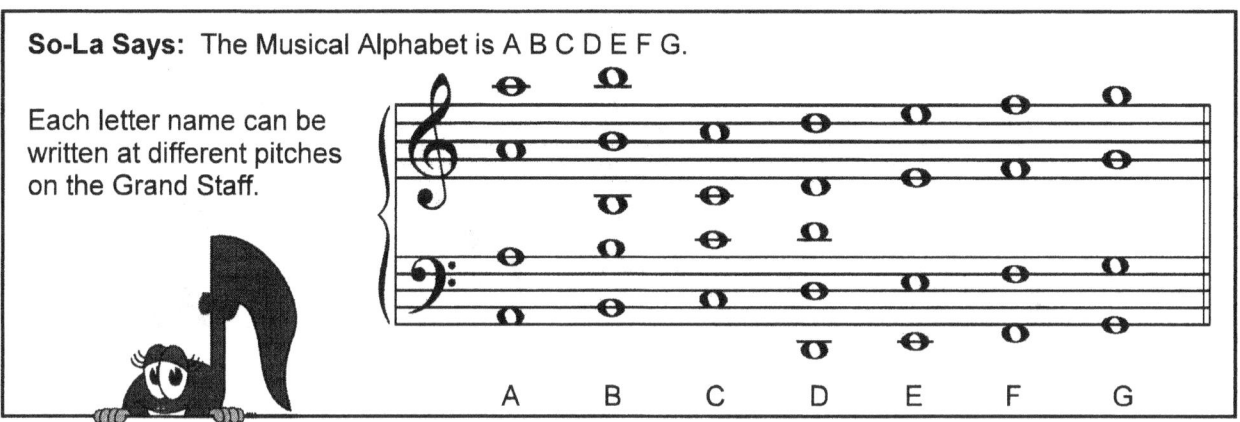

1. a) Name each note.
   b) In each measure, circle the 2 notes that are written at the same pitch but in the alternate clef.

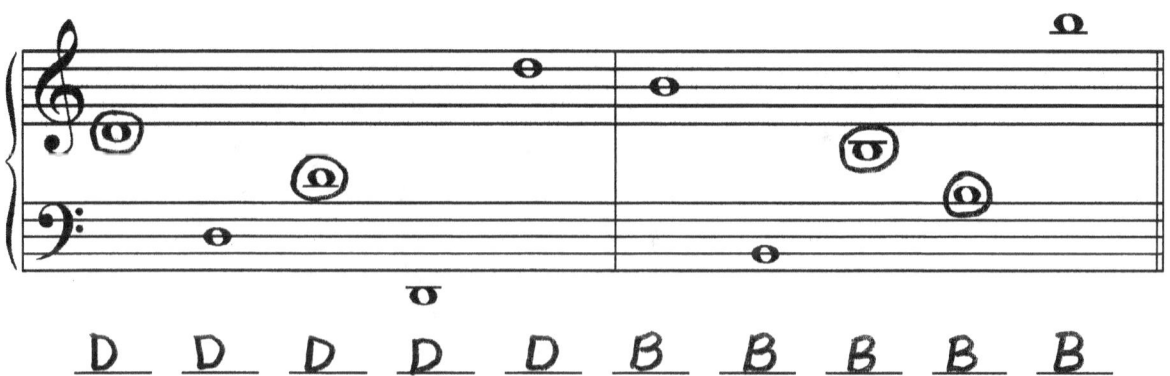

D D D D D B B B B B

♫ **Ti-Do Tip:** An Octave is the distance of 8 notes. The distance between one note and the next note with the same letter name (going up or going down) is an Octave (8 notes).

2. In each measure, write four notes for each letter name. Use whole notes. Each note must be at a different pitch.

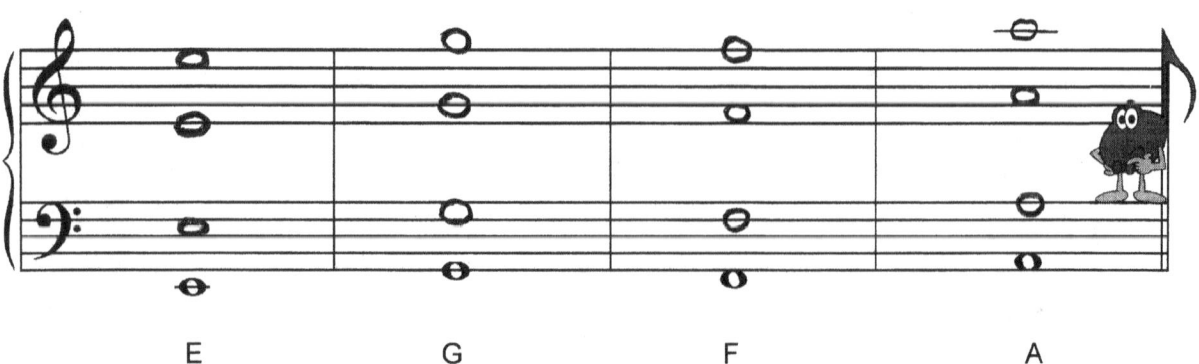

E G F A

C MAJOR SCALE (Use after Prep 1 Rudiments Page 79)

A **Major scale** is a series of 8 notes or degrees that move by step (from one letter name to the next letter name). A scale can be written going up one octave (ascending 8 notes) or going down one octave (descending 8 notes).

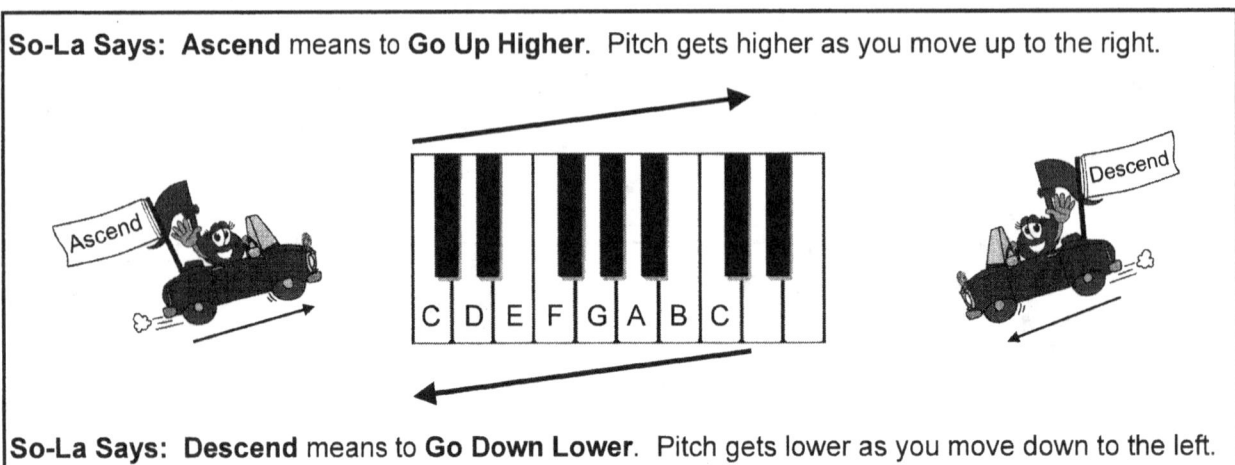

So-La Says: **Ascend** means to **Go Up Higher**. Pitch gets higher as you move up to the right.

So-La Says: **Descend** means to **Go Down Lower**. Pitch gets lower as you move down to the left.

1. a) Name the notes of the ascending C Major scale.
   b) Draw a line from each note to the corresponding key on the keyboard (at the correct pitch).
   c) Name each key of the C Major scale directly on the keyboard.

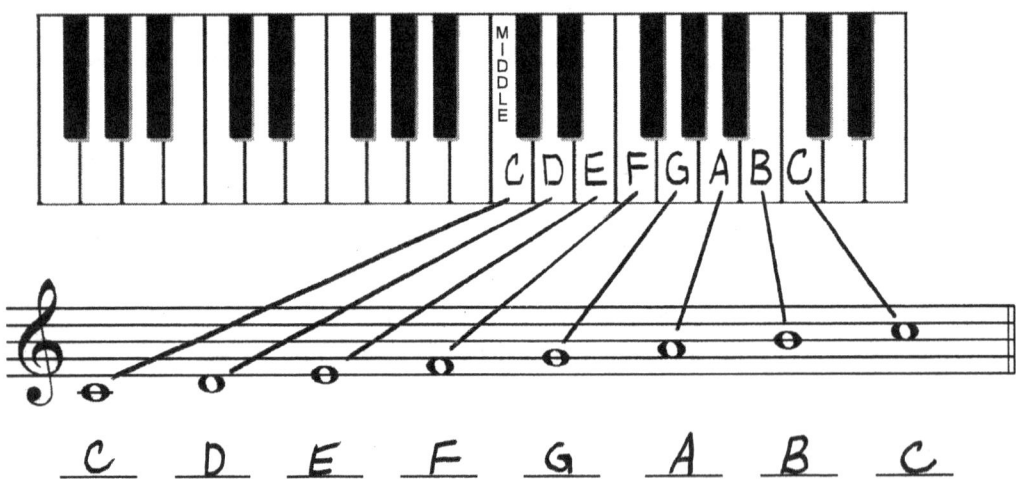

C   D   E   F   G   A   B   C

♪ **Ti-Do Time:** PLAY the C Major scale ascending. PLAY the C Major scale descending.

LISTEN as your teacher plays the C Major scale ascending or descending.

Identify if the notes are stepping higher (ascending) or if the notes are stepping lower (descending).

C MAJOR SCALE and the TONIC (Use after Prep 1 Rudiments Page 79)

The starting note ($\hat{1}$, or first note) of the ascending Scale is called the **Tonic Note**. The ending note or last note $\hat{8}$ ($\hat{1}$) of the ascending Scale is also the Tonic Note as it uses the same letter name.

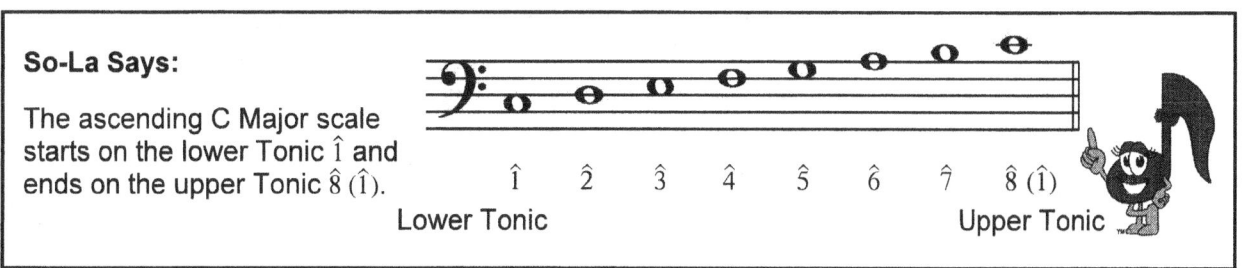

So-La Says: The ascending C Major scale starts on the lower Tonic $\hat{1}$ and ends on the upper Tonic $\hat{8}$ ($\hat{1}$).

♪ **Ti-Do Tip:** A special " ^ " sign (a circumflex, "hat" or caret sign) is used above the degree numbers of a scale so that you do not confuse the scale degree numbers with finger numbers!

1. Write the letter names of the ascending C Major scale above the numbers.

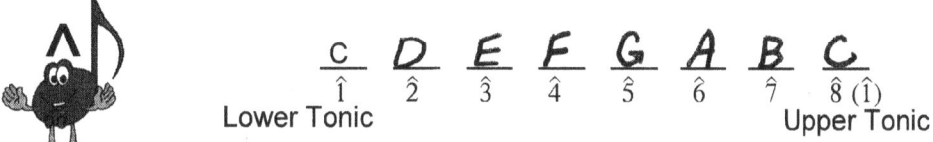

2. Write the C Major scale ascending in the Treble Clef. Use whole notes. Circle each Tonic note.

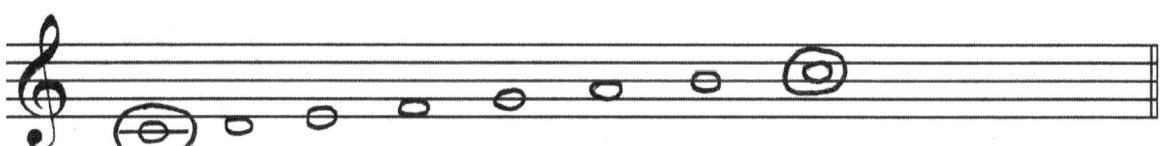

So-La Says: The descending C Major scale starts on the upper Tonic $\hat{8}$ ($\hat{1}$) and ends on the lower Tonic $\hat{1}$.

3. Write the letter names of the descending C Major scale above the numbers.

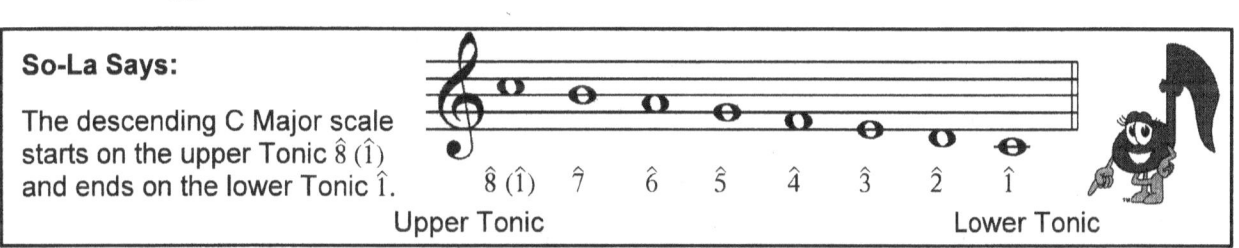

4. Write the C Major scale descending in the Bass Clef. Use whole notes. Circle each Tonic note.

A MINOR SCALE, NATURAL FORM (Use after Prep 1 Rudiments Page 97)

A **minor scale** is a series of 8 notes that move by step (from one letter name to the next). Each Major scale has a **relative minor scale** that is 3 steps below the Tonic note of the Major scale.

C Major scale has no sharps or flats. The relative a minor scale also has no sharps or flats.

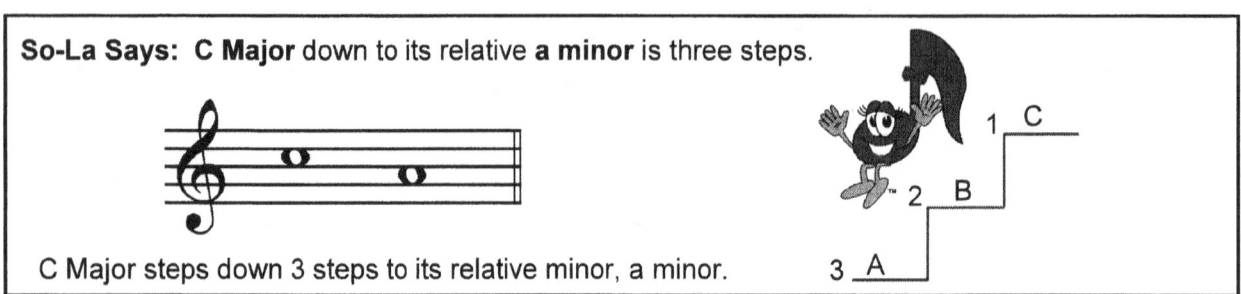

So-La Says: C Major down to its relative **a minor** is three steps.

C Major steps down 3 steps to its relative minor, a minor.

♪ **Ti-Do Tip:** There are 3 forms of minor scales: Natural Form, Harmonic Form and Melodic Form. The **natural form** of the minor scale has the SAME notes as its relative Major scale.

1. Check (✓) the correct answer.
   a) The relative minor of C Major is ☑ a minor or ☐ C Major.
   b) The relative Major of a minor is ☐ a minor or ☑ C Major.

So-La Says:

The **a minor scale, natural form,** can ascend (go up higher) or descend (go down lower).

2. a) Name the notes of the ascending a minor scale, natural form.
   b) Draw a line from each note to the corresponding key on the keyboard (at the correct pitch).
   c) Name each key of the a minor scale directly on the keyboard.

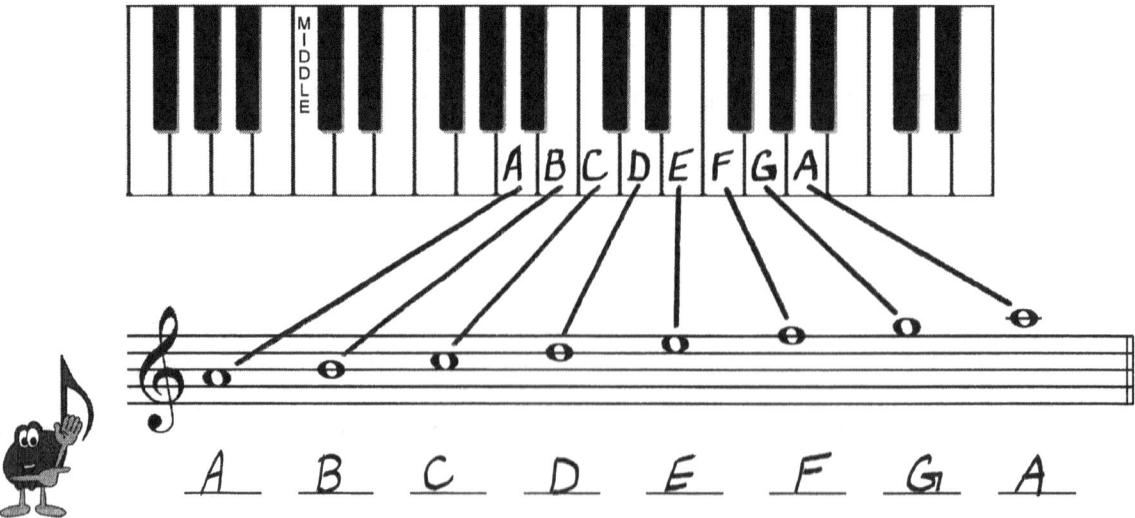

A   B   C   D   E   F   G   A

A MINOR SCALE, NATURAL FORM, and the TONIC (Use after Prep 1 Rudiments Page 97)

A **Major scale** may be written using an **Upper Case letter name** (C Major scale).
A **minor scale** may be written using a **lower case letter name** (a minor scale).

So-La Says:

The ascending a minor scale starts on the lower Tonic $\hat{1}$ and ends on the upper Tonic $\hat{8}$ ($\hat{1}$).

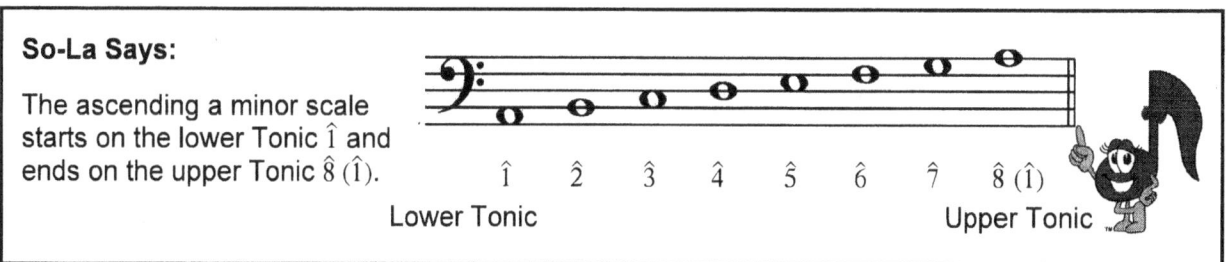

♪ **Ti-Do Tip:** Letter Names are always written using Upper Case Letters (Capital Letters). Always use an **Upper Case Letter** to identify the Letter Name of the **Tonic Note**.

1. Write the letter names of the ascending a minor scale, natural form, above the numbers.

2. Write the a minor scale, natural form, ascending in the Treble Clef. Use whole notes. Circle each Tonic note.

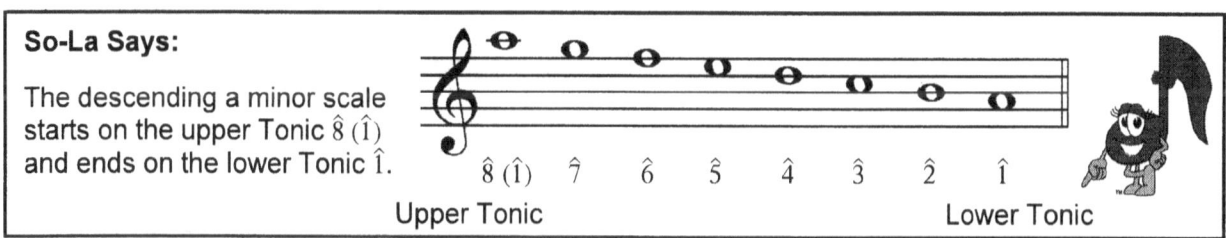

So-La Says:

The descending a minor scale starts on the upper Tonic $\hat{8}$ ($\hat{1}$) and ends on the lower Tonic $\hat{1}$.

3. Write the letter names of the descending a minor scale, natural form, above the numbers.

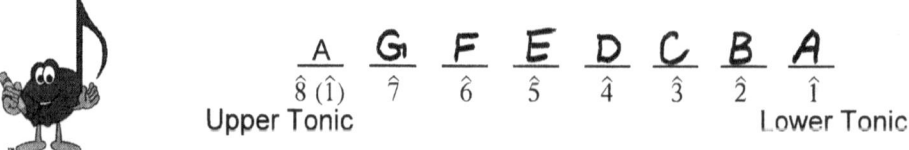

4. Write the a minor scale, natural form, descending in the Bass Clef. Use whole notes. Circle each Tonic note.

MUSICAL TERMS and SIGNS (Use after Prep 1 Rudiments Page 102)

Dynamics are signs that indicate the volume at which the music is played.

Dynamic Terms	Dynamic Symbols or Signs	Definition
crescendo	cresc. or <	becoming louder
diminuendo	dim. or >	becoming softer
decrescendo	decresc. or >	becoming softer
forte	*f*	loud
mezzo forte	*mf*	medium loud (moderately loud)
mezzo piano	*mp*	medium soft (moderately soft)
piano	*p*	soft

1. Rearrange the following dynamic signs in order from softest to loudest.

   mf   *mp*   *f*   *p*

   (Softest) __*p*__ __*mp*__ __*mf*__ __*f*__ (Loudest)

Articulation refers to the way that a note can be played. Different types of sound are created by using different articulation (touch).

Articulation Terms	Articulation Mark	Definition
accent	>	a stressed note
staccato	.	sharply detached
legato		play smoothly and connected (smooth)
slur	⌢	curved line indicating to play notes legato

2. Analyze the following melody by answering the questions below.

   a) Identify the articulation mark in measure 1. __slur__
   b) Identify the articulation marks in measure 2. __staccato__
   c) Identify the articulation mark in measure 3. __accent__

MELODY WRITING (Use after Prep 1 Workbook Page 107)

A **Melody** is a sequence of single notes that form a piece of music or song. A melody may go up or down or have repeated notes. A melody also has a rhythm. Together they create a composition.

♫ **Ti-Do Tip:** A melody is written based on the notes of a scale. A melody usually ends on the Tonic note. The melody below is based on the C Major Scale and ends on the Tonic note C.

1. Complete the melody writing exercise by copying the steps below.

    a) Write the Rhythm (rhythmic pattern) above the Treble Staff.
    b) Write the Melody (melodic idea) on the Treble Staff.
    c) Write the Basic Beat (2 quarter notes per measure) below the Treble Staff.

So-La Says: Look at the above melody, "Ti-Do Steps".

Sing the melody that you see. Match what you see to what you hear.
Play the melody on your instrument to HEAR what you SEE.

♫ **Ti-Do Tip:** When composing a melody, there may be **more than one correct answer**.

2. Compose a melody in measures 2 and 3. Use the given rhythm. Use repeated notes or notes that move by step or skip. Sing or play your composition.

MOTIVE - A MUSICAL IDEA (Use after Prep 1 Workbook Page 108)

A melody has a **Motive**. A motive is a short rhythmic and/or melodic idea that is like planting a musical seed. A motive can be repeated (the same or in different ways) as the music grows.

♫ **Ti-Do Tip:** When a motive is written at the same pitch with the same rhythmic pattern and melodic idea, it is called **Repetition**. It is a "copy-cat" of the original motive.

1. This melody is in C Major. Compose a melody in measures 2, 3 and 4. Use the given rhythm.

    a) Repeat the motive (repetition of the rhythmic and melodic idea) from measure 1 in measure 2.
    b) Compose a melody in measure 3. Use repeated notes or notes that move by step or skip.
    c) Compose a melody in measure 4. End on the Tonic note C (degree î of C Major scale).

(one possible answer)

 **So-La Says:** A melody that ends on the Tonic note (î) sounds final or finished. The Tonic note, scale degree î, is called a STABLE degree.

2. The melody below is in C Major. Check (✓) the correct answer.

		Yes	or	No
a)	The motive is repeated in measure 2.	☐		✓
b)	Repeated notes are played in measure 3.	✓		☐
c)	The melody contains ledger line notes.	✓		☐
d)	The Tonic note C is played 4 times.	☐		✓
e)	The melody ends on a stable degree (î).	✓		☐

IMAGINE, COMPOSE, EXPLORE (Use after Prep 1 Workbook Page 113)

Composing means to create music. We can compose music by making up a melody and playing it on an instrument, or by making up words for a song and singing it.

♪ Imagine the music telling a story or idea. The title (written at the top) describes the composition.
♪ Compose the music to express your musical idea. Your piece may be happy, sad, funny, etc.
♪ Explore the music. Add "So-La Sparkles" using dynamics and articulation to enhance the sound.

So-La Says: First compose freely without writing anything down. Use a recording device (such as your phone, computer or video camera) to record yourself.

Use the recording to assist you in writing out your composition. Use different dynamics, articulation and tempo to create different sounds and adventures.

1. For each of the following: compose a melody in measures 2, 3 & 4. Use the given rhythm.

    a) Imagine what the motive (musical idea) is about. Complete the title at the top of the piece.
    b) Compose a melody using repeated notes or notes that move by step. End on the Tonic 1̂ note.
    c) Explore the music. Add "So-La Sparkles" using dynamics and articulation.

ANALYSIS and SIGHT READING (Use after Prep 1 Workbook Page 115)

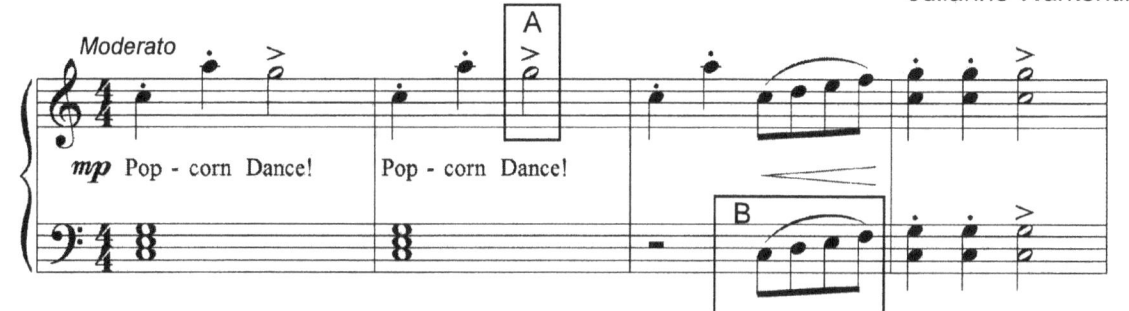

1. Analyze the piece of music by answering the questions below.

   a) Identify the C Major triad in measure 1 as solid or broken. **Solid**

   b) Circle the pattern of notes in measure 1 and measure 2. (**same**) or different

   c) Explain the articulation mark at the letter A. **accent - stressed note**

   d) Circle the direction for the notes at the letter B. (**stepping up**) or stepping down

   e) Circle the descending C Major scale (C to C) that begins in measure 5 and ends in measure 6.

 ♫ **Ti-Do Time:**

IDENTIFY the Time Signature. CLAP the rhythm in the Treble Clef. Count out loud. Tap a steady Basic Beat with your foot. CLAP and count the rhythm in the Bass Clef.

So-La Says: Sight Reading is the reading and performing of a piece of music or of a song in music notation that the performer has not seen before.

PLAY (Sight Read) the "Popcorn Dance" on your instrument. Sing the words "Popcorn Dance" as the Popcorn pops and dances!

MUSIC HISTORY - TIME PERIODS and INSTRUMENTS (Medieval to Classical)

♪ **Ti-Do Tip:** For as long as humans have been on this earth, so has music! Music has always been an important part of everyday life.

History has divided music into different **Time Periods**.

The **Medieval Period** is music from the years around **500 to 1450**. During this period in music history, the most common type of music was the Plainsong (or Plain Chant). This was vocal music sung by the Priests during the Roman Catholic Church Services.

The **Lyre** is considered to be the main ancestor of the harp. Lyres often had different numbers of strings. A 5-stringed Lyre could be tuned to a Pentascale.

1. Name the period from 500 - 1450. __Medieval Period__

The **Renaissance Period** is music from around **1450 to 1600**. Renaissance is French for "rebirth". The Renaissance period was a time of discoveries and new beginnings. Music was a big part of Church services, the Courts of the Nobility, and also in the homes of everyday people!

William Shakespeare wrote about the **Recorder** in his play "Hamlet". Instrument makers began making recorders in various sizes with a range of a 6th to an octave.

2. Name the period from 1450 - 1600. __Renaissance Period__

The **Baroque Period** is music from around the years **1600 to 1750**. Music was very important to the Kings, Queens and Monarchs who ruled over their countries. Many Courts had their own musicians and their own Composer (to write and perform music for special events and gatherings).

The **Harp** was very popular as it could play low bass notes as well as higher pitched harmonies. Harp Strings were made of "gut" (from the intestines of a sheep or goat).

3. Name the period from 1600 - 1750. __Baroque Period__

The **Classical Period** is from **1750 to 1825**. This was the time of the "Industrial Revolution", when machines became popular. Machines helped make it easier for instruments to be made and for music to be printed. Instruments became more affordable - they weren't just for the rich.

By the age of 5, Wolfgang Amadeus Mozart could already play the **Violin**! The Violin Bow is a wooden stick strung end to end with strands of horsehair.

4. Name the period from 1750 - 1825. __Classical Period__

MUSIC HISTORY - TIME PERIODS and INSTRUMENTS (Romantic to Today)

♫ **Ti-Do Tip:** Marching Bands are popular today, especially in schools and at sporting events. Did you know that there have been Marching Bands for thousands of years?

As early as the 7th Century BC, Ancient Egyptians marched to the sounds of drums and trumpets!

The **Romantic Period** is music from **around 1825 to 1900**. Music during this period had lots of expression and dynamics. People enjoyed going to Concerts to hear musicians and orchestras perform. The telephone and the car were also invented during this period in history!

In the early 1800s, Beethoven's **Grand Piano** had a range of 6 octaves. By the middle 1800s, the Grand Piano used by Liszt had a span of 7 octaves.

1. Name the period from 1825 - 1900. _Romantic Period_

The **20th and 21st Century Period** is music from around **1900 to today**. This is also called the Modern or Contemporary Period. Music began to be recorded and then played on the Radio. Electronic music (using computers) helped create new styles of music.

The **Electronic Keyboard** (called a synthesizer or digital piano) is often capable of recreating the sounds of different instruments. It requires electricity to be played.

2. Name the period from 1900 - today. _20th and 21st Century Period_

---

3. Draw a line to match the Music Time Periods with their correct dates.

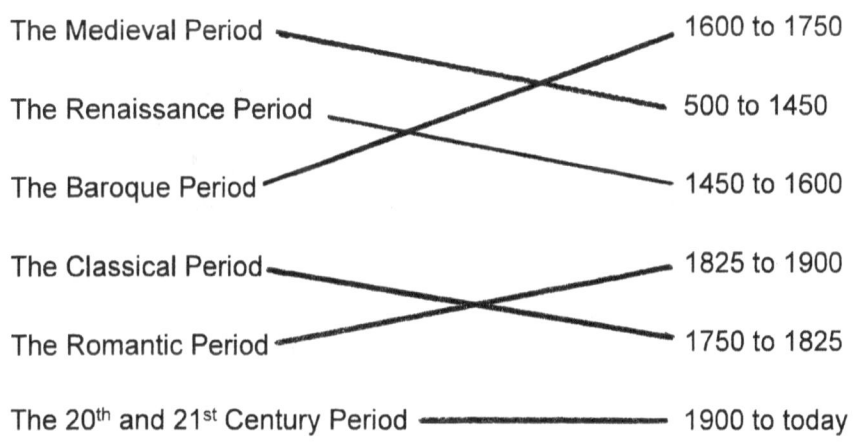

4. Name one instrument from each period.

lyre	_recorder_	_harp_	_violin_	_grand piano_	_electronic keyboard_
Medieval	Renaissance	Baroque	Classical	Romantic	20th/21st Century

Ultimate Music Theory
Preparatory Level Theory Exam

Total Score: ___/100

The Ultimate Music Theory™ Rudiments Workbooks, Supplemental Workbooks and Exams prepare students for successful completion of the Royal Conservatory of Music Theory Levels.

1. a) Name the following notes.
   b) Draw a line from each note to the corresponding key on the keyboard (at the correct pitch).
   c) Name the key directly on the keyboard.

___/10

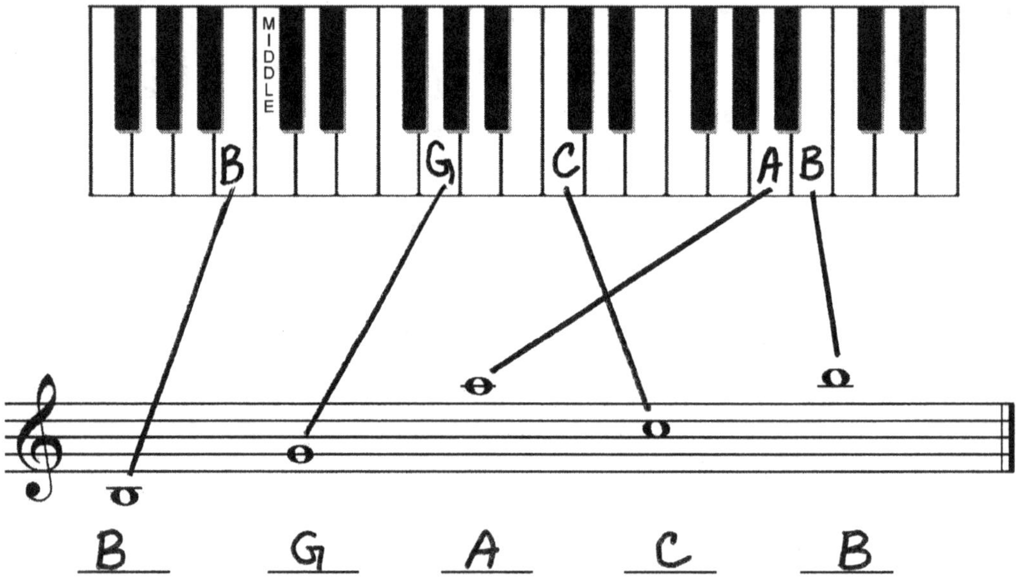

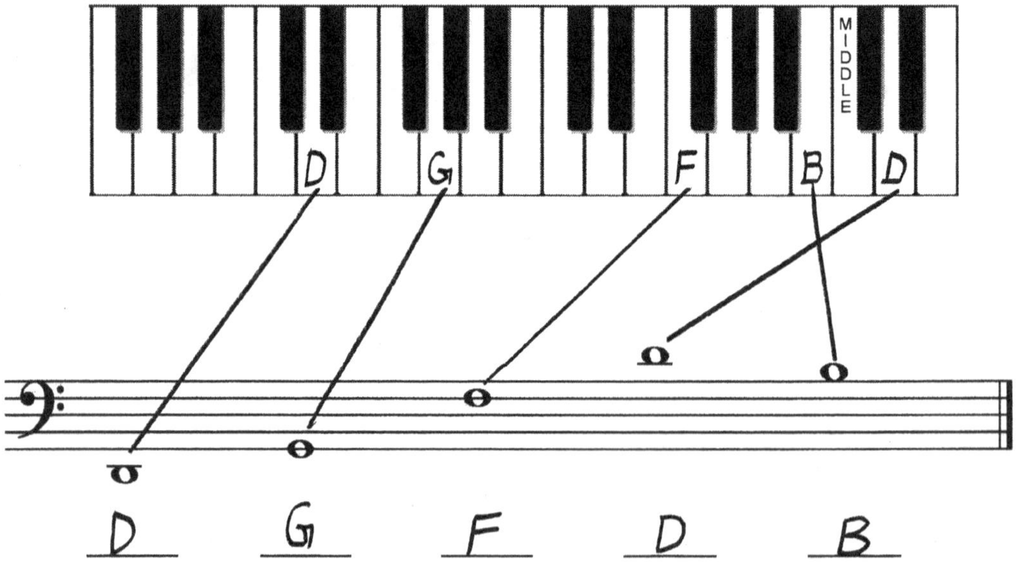

B G A C B

D G F D B

UltimateMusicTheory.com © Copyright 2017 Gloryland Publishing. All Rights Reserved. 30

Ultimate Music Theory
Preparatory Level Theory Exam

2. a) On the Grand Staff, draw four different pitched notes for each letter name. Use whole notes.

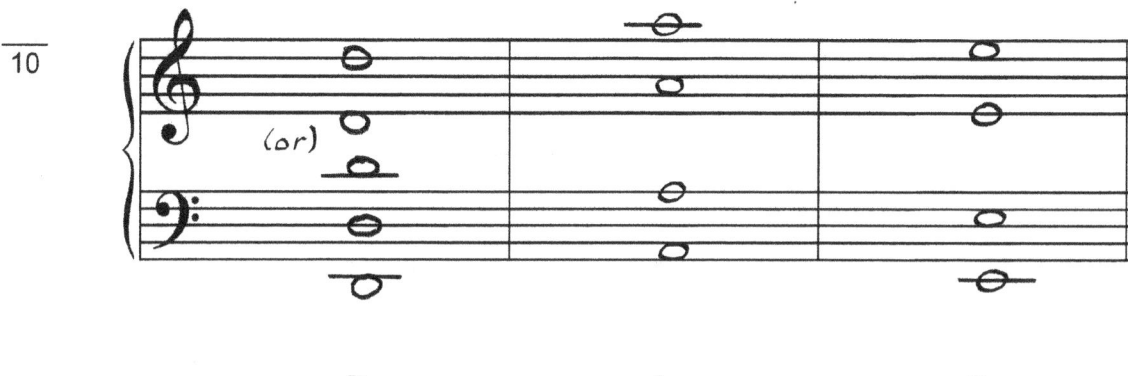

          D   A   E

b) Draw a Brace (Bracket) at the beginning of the Grand Staff.
c) Use a Bar Line to divide the Staff into 2 measures.

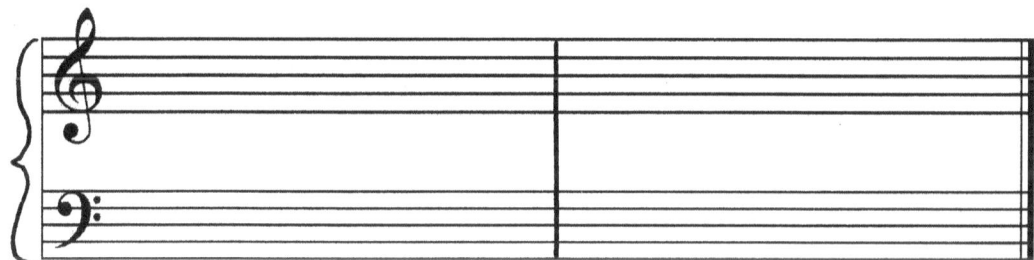

d) Name the following whole notes.

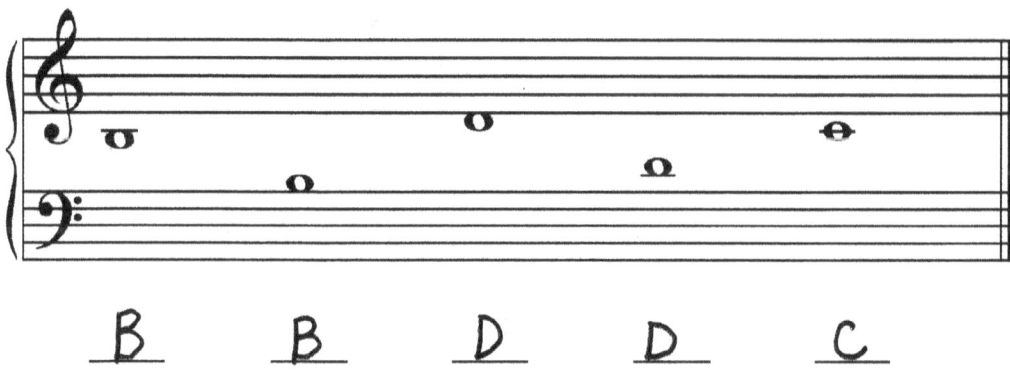

     B   B   D   D   C

Ultimate Music Theory
Preparatory Level Theory Exam

3. a) Identify the patterns between each pair of notes as:
      same line, same space, step up, step down, skip up or skip down.

/10

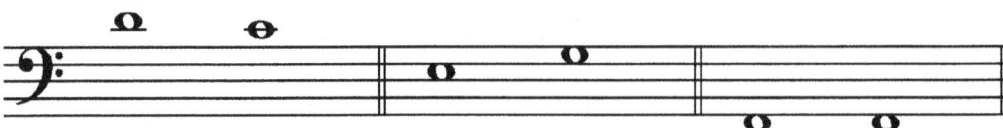

Pattern: step down   skip up   same space

Pattern: same line   step up   skip down

b) Following the Direction Arrow, draw a whole note a step up (stepping higher) or a step down (stepping lower) from each given note.
c) Name the notes.

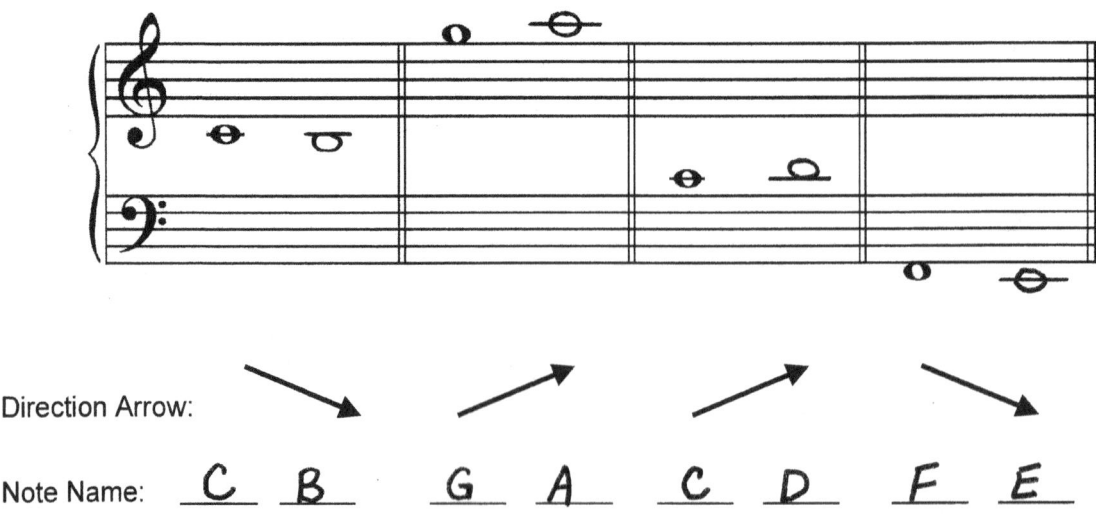

Direction Arrow: ↘   ↗   ↗   ↘

Note Name: C B   G A   C D   F E

Ultimate Music Theory
Preparatory Level Theory Exam

4. a) Draw a rest that has the same value as each note.
    b) Name the type of note/rest (whole, half, quarter or eighth).

quarter   half

whole   eighth

c) Draw one rest that is equal in value to the combined value of the given rests.

UltimateMusicTheory.com © Copyright 2017 Gloryland Publishing. All Rights Reserved.

Ultimate Music Theory
Preparatory Level Theory Exam

5. a) Draw the correct clef for each note. Use a Treble Clef or a Bass Clef.

___
10

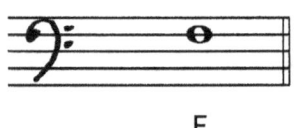
F

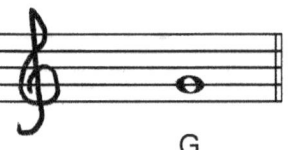
G

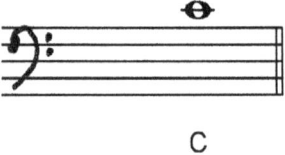
C

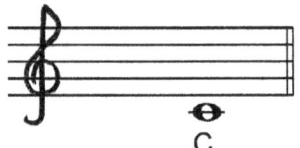
C

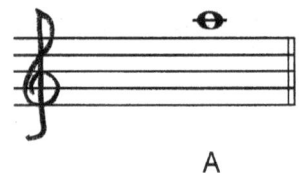
A

E

c) Draw one note that is equal in value to the combined value of the given notes.

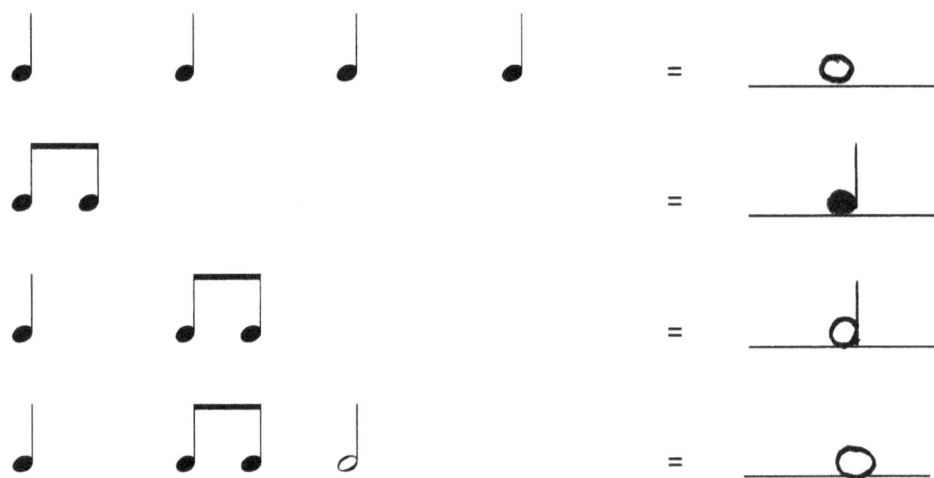

Ultimate Music Theory
Preparatory Level Theory Exam

6. a) Write the correct Time Signature below each bracket.

b) Add bar lines to complete the following rhythms.

Ultimate Music Theory
Preparatory Level Theory Exam

7. a) Write the C Major scale descending (going down) one octave. Use whole notes. Circle each Tonic Note.

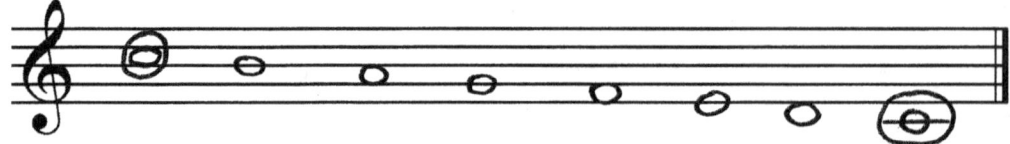

b) Write the a minor scale, natural form, ascending (going up) one octave. Use whole notes. Circle each Tonic Note.

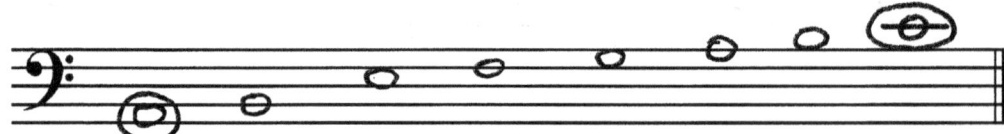

c) Write the a minor scale, natural form, descending (going down) one octave. Use whole notes. Circle each Tonic Note.

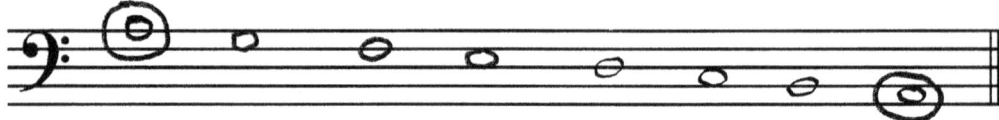

d) Add a Treble Clef or a Bass Clef at the beginning of the following staff to form the C Major scale (ascending).

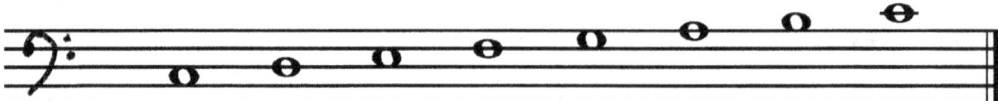

e) Add a Treble Clef or a Bass Clef at the beginning of the following staff to form the a minor scale, natural form (descending).

Ultimate Music Theory
Preparatory Level Theory Exam

8. Match each triad name with the correct triad.

__10__

a minor Triad, Solid (Blocked), in the Bass Clef   __d__

C Major Triad, Solid (Blocked), in the Treble Clef   __a__

a minor Triad, Broken ascending (going up), in the Bass Clef   __b__

C Major Triad, Broken ascending (going up), in the Treble Clef   __c__

a minor Triad, Broken ascending (going up), in the Treble Clef   __f__

a minor Triad, Solid (Blocked), in the Treble Clef   __e__

Ultimate Music Theory
Preparatory Level Theory Exam

9. Circle the correct sign or symbol for each of the following definitions.

10

Definition	Sign or Symbol		
detached	(♩.)	or	♩>
moderately loud	*mp*	or	(*mf*)
becoming louder	(cresc.)	or	dim.
becoming louder	>	or	(<)
loud	(*f*)	or	*p*
play the notes *legato*	(♩♩♩ slur)	or	♩.
becoming softer	cresc.	or	(decresc.)
a stressed note	(♩>)	or	*f*
indicates the end of a piece	‖	or	(final barline)
moderately soft	(*mp*)	or	*p*

Ultimate Music Theory
Preparatory Level Theory Exam

10. Analyze the following piece of music by answering the questions below.

Cupcakes and Sprinkles
S. McKibbon

a) Name the title of this piece. **Cupcakes and Sprinkles**

b) Name the composer of this piece. **S. McKibbon**

c) Add the Time Signature directly on the music.

d) Explain the meaning of "*mf*". **mezzo forte - moderately loud**

e) Name the notes at the letters: A. **G**   B. **C**

f) Circle the direction for the notes at the letter C.   stepping up   or   **(stepping down)**

g) Circle the pattern of the notes at the letter D.   same line   or   **(same space)**

h) Circle the name of the sign at the letter E.   accent   or   **(staccato)**

i) Circle the name of the triad at the letter F.   **(C Major)**   or   a minor

j) Identify the number of slurs in this piece. **two**

UltimateMusicTheory.com © Copyright 2017 Gloryland Publishing. All Rights Reserved. 39

Ultimate Music Theory Certificate

_____

has successfully completed all the requirements of the

Music Theory Preparatory Level

_____   _____
Music Teacher   *Date*

Enriching Lives Through Music Education

www.ingramcontent.com/pod-product-compliance
Lightning Source LLC
Chambersburg PA
CBHW080023130526
44591CB00036B/2635